Made in the USA
Monee, IL
08 July 2022

99337918R00063